MW01101856

NORKAM SECONDARY SCHOOL
730 - 12th STREET
KAMLOOPS, BC V2B 3C1
PH:(250) 376-1272
FAX (250) 376-9142

COMPACT *Research*

Teenage Suicide

Teenage Problems

ReferencePoint
Press®

San Diego, CA

Other books in the Compact Research Teenage Problems set:

Teenage Alcoholism
Teenage Drug Abuse
Teenage Eating Disorders
Teenage Mental Illness
Teenage Sex and Pregnancy

*For a complete list of titles please visit www.referencepointpress.com.

COMPACT *Research*

Teenage
Suicide

Peggy J. Parks

Teenage Problems

ReferencePoint
Press®

San Diego, CA

For more information, contact:
ReferencePoint Press, Inc.
PO Box 27779
San Diego, CA 92198
www.ReferencePointPress.com

Picture credits:
Cover: iStockphoto.com and Thinkstock/Comstock
Maury Aaseng: 32–34, 46–48, 60–61, 73–75
AP Images: 18
iStockphoto.com: 14

LIBRARY OF CONGRESS CATALOGING-IN-PUBLICATION DATA

Parks, Peggy J., 1951–
  Teenage suicide / by Peggy J. Parks.
    p. cm. — (Compact research series)
  Includes bibliographical references and index.
  ISBN-13: 978-1-60152-156-9 (hardback : alk. paper)
  ISBN-10: 1-60152-156-1 (hardback : alk. paper)
  1. Teenagers—Suicidal behavior—United States—Juvenile literature. 2. Bullying—United States—Juvenile literature. I. Title.
  HV6546.P374 2012
  362.280835—dc22
                                  2010047530

Contents

Foreword

> "**Where is the knowledge we have lost in information?**"
>
> —T.S. Eliot, "The Rock."

As modern civilization continues to evolve, its ability to create, store, distribute, and access information expands exponentially. The explosion of information from all media continues to increase at a phenomenal rate. By 2020 some experts predict the worldwide information base will double every 73 days. While access to diverse sources of information and perspectives is paramount to any democratic society, information alone cannot help people gain knowledge and understanding. Information must be organized and presented clearly and succinctly in order to be understood. The challenge in the digital age becomes not the creation of information, but how best to sort, organize, enhance, and present information.

ReferencePoint Press developed the *Compact Research* series with this challenge of the information age in mind. More than any other subject area today, researching current issues can yield vast, diverse, and unqualified information that can be intimidating and overwhelming for even the most advanced and motivated researcher. The *Compact Research* series offers a compact, relevant, intelligent, and conveniently organized collection of information covering a variety of current topics ranging from illegal immigration and deforestation to diseases such as anorexia and meningitis.

The series focuses on three types of information: objective single-author narratives, opinion-based primary source quotations, and facts and statistics. The clearly written objective narratives provide context and reliable background information. Primary source quotes are carefully selected and cited, exposing the reader to differing points of view. And facts and statistics sections aid the reader in evaluating perspectives. Presenting these key types of information creates a richer, more balanced learning experience.

For better understanding and convenience, the series enhances information by organizing it into narrower topics and adding design features that make it easy for a reader to identify desired content. For example, in *Compact Research: Illegal Immigration*, a chapter covering the economic impact of illegal immigration has an objective narrative explaining the various ways the economy is impacted, a balanced section of numerous primary source quotes on the topic, followed by facts and full-color illustrations to encourage evaluation of contrasting perspectives.

The ancient Roman philosopher Lucius Annaeus Seneca wrote, "It is quality rather than quantity that matters." More than just a collection of content, the *Compact Research* series is simply committed to creating, finding, organizing, and presenting the most relevant and appropriate amount of information on a current topic in a user-friendly style that invites, intrigues, and fosters understanding.

Teenage Suicide at a Glance

Severity of Problem

According to the Centers for Disease Control and Prevention, suicide is the third leading cause of death for teenagers, with an average of 1,841 teens killing themselves each year.

Suicide Methods

Firearm suicide is most prevalent among teenage boys, while girls most often die from suffocation, usually by hanging.

Warning Signs

Teens who are suicidal often undergo personality changes, withdraw from friends and family, lose interest in activities they enjoy, and/or make remarks about wanting to die.

Why Teens Commit Suicide

An estimated 90 percent of teens who take their own lives suffered from depression, substance abuse, or another mental health disorder.

Copycat Suicide

Studies have suggested vulnerable teenagers may be influenced to kill themselves after reading or hearing about other teens who have taken their own lives.

The Role of Bullying

Bullying has been shown to cause teens extreme distress, but whether it can be considered a cause of suicide is controversial.

Preventing Teen Suicide

Since suicidal teens often suffer from mental health issues such as depression and substance abuse, treatment for those problems can help reduce suicidal thoughts.

Overview

66While many teens have these emotional ups and downs, for some, the downs can be fatal. Sadly, every year in the United States, thousands of teenagers are unable to deal with these feelings and commit suicide.99

—American Academy of Pediatrics, an organization that is committed to the physical health, mental health, and well-being of all children, adolescents, and young adults.

66Suicide ended their suffering at the cost of leaving a dark mark on the life of everyone who cared for them. Parents and close friends never get over the death of a child.99

—Jim Wellborn, child and adolescent psychologist from Brentwood, Tennessee.

On February 8, 2009, at about 2:30 in the morning, a horrific crash occurred in Bartow, Florida. The car, driven by 17-year-old Candra Rittenhouse, was traveling at a high rate of speed when it suddenly swerved off the road, flew through the air, and slammed into a utility pole, snapping the pole in half. Neither Rittenhouse nor her passenger, 16-year-old Sara Kay Smith, was wearing a seatbelt, and both were thrown out of the vehicle. The girls were airlifted to a hospital in Tampa, where Rittenhouse died during surgery. Although Smith was seriously injured, she survived—and what she told police detectives shocked the girls' parents. She explained that the crash was not an accident but a planned event, part of a suicide pact that she and Rittenhouse had made the day before. "We wanted to die together,"[1] she said.

Rittenhouse's parents refused to believe that their daughter would intentionally kill herself. She was doing well in school, had won blue ribbons for her cooking, and aspired to become a chef someday. "She was a happy girl," says her stepfather. "You won't get anybody to believe that this was something Candra wanted."[2] Detectives formed a different conclusion, however. After completing their investigation, they were convinced that Smith was telling the truth. Autopsy results showed that Rittenhouse had no alcohol or drugs in her system, and at the scene of the crash there were no skid marks or other signs to indicate that she had made any attempt to stop. As a result, investigators determined that Rittenhouse had deliberately crashed into the utility pole, and the cause of her death was changed from accidental injuries to suicide.

How Serious a Problem Is Teenage Suicide?

The way Rittenhouse killed herself is rare among teenagers—but teen suicide is not so rare. According to a May 2010 report by the Centers for Disease Control and Prevention (CDC), a total of 131,000 young people aged 12 to 19 died in the United States between 1999 and 2006. Most of the deaths resulted from accidental injuries, with the majority being from motor vehicle crashes. Homicide was the second leading cause of death, and suicide was third. Every year, an average of 1,841 American teenagers deliberately take their own lives. In fact, more teenagers die by suicide than from heart disease, cancer, birth defects, influenza, pneumonia, and AIDS *combined.*

Teen suicide is a serious problem not only in the United States but in many other countries as well. Young people all over the world take their own lives, as the advisory group Parliamentary Assembly of the Council of Europe explains: "Teenage suicide has become a serious public-health issue. The importance of the problem is often underestimated,

> **More teenagers die by suicide than from heart disease, cancer, birth defects, influenza, pneumonia, and AIDS *combined.***

yet there are tens of thousands of suicides every year."[3] The World Health Organization estimates that 100,000 adolescents worldwide die each year by taking their own lives. Yet according to researchers from Sweden and

China, suicide statistics are underreported for cultural and religious reasons. Also, in many countries suicides are often misclassified (or masked) as other causes of death, so the true global picture of teenage suicide is likely much grimmer than is known.

How They Try to Die

Both male and female teenagers commit suicide, although there are some behavioral differences. Girls, for instance, attempt suicide at least 3 times more often than boys, but boys succeed in killing themselves far more often. The CDC states that of the reported suicides among youth and young adults aged 10 to 24, more than 80 percent of the deaths were males. The likely reason for this, according to the Substance Abuse and Mental Health Services Administration, is that teenage boys may be more motivated actually to die than girls. The agency explains: "Young women often attempt suicide by overdosing on drugs or cutting themselves—methods which offer more opportunities for rescue. Young men often use firearms, hanging, or jumping from heights—methods which usually cause instant death and offer no chance to intervene."[4]

Firearm suicide is most prevalent among teenage boys, with more than half of male teens shooting themselves to death. Although girls also use firearms, most die from suffocation (most often by hanging)—which is a major change from the 1990s. The CDC states that in 1991, teenage girls and boys committed suicide with firearms at about the same rate. As of 2006, the most recent year for which comprehensive data are available, suffocation was the most prevalent method of suicide for females aged 10 to 24, followed by firearms. Among males the reverse is true: Firearms are the number one means of suicide, with suffocation being the second-most common method.

Teens at Risk

Many teens are at risk for suicidal thinking and behavior, but some have a much higher risk than others. According to the CDC, "A combination of individual, relational, community, and societal factors contribute to the risk of suicide."[5] Risk factors are characteristics or situations that have been associated with suicide but may or may not be direct causes. Some of these include a family history of suicide, feelings of hopelessness, and barriers to accessing mental health treatment, along with impulsive or aggressive tendencies, a history of running away from home, and previous suicide attempts. These and other risk factors are determined through various means such as studies that are performed after death, which are known as psychological autopsies.

According to Madelyn S. Gould, who is a professor of clinical psychiatry at Columbia University's College of Physicians and Surgeons, psychological autopsies can help scientists better understand the factors that led to a teen's suicide. She writes:

> " Another potential warning sign is if a teen starts meticulously cleaning and organizing his or her room in order to select cherished possessions to be given away. "

> These studies reconstruct circumstances surrounding a suicide by talking with family members, friends, and sometimes employers and health care providers. Psychological autopsy studies also often involve a review of medical records. Using this, a person's background, developmental history, symptoms, illnesses, stressors, and social circumstances help form a qualitative understanding of the person prior to suicide.[6]

Psychological autopsies can provide scientists with an in-depth understanding of teens who have killed themselves, and are also useful for identifying potential risk factors for other young people.

When Kids Are Hurting

According to the American Academy of Child & Adolescent Psychiatry (AACAP), a number of warning signs may be exhibited by teens who are having suicidal thoughts. For instance, many develop personality changes such as withdrawing from their friends and family members, easily becoming restless and frustrated, feeling tired much of the time, and losing interest in activities they usually enjoy. They may begin binge eating and have trouble sleeping and concentrating, which causes a marked decline in schoolwork and grades. Another potential warning sign is if a teen starts meticulously cleaning and organizing his or her

Suicide is the third leading cause of death among U.S. teenagers, behind accidental injuries (mainly car accidents) and homicides. Although various events might cause a teenager to contemplate or carry out suicide, depression is considered the strongest contributor.

room in order to select cherished possessions to be given away.

Young people may also say things that could indicate suicidal thinking. For instance, a teen may complain of feeling like a bad person who does not deserve to live, or say that people would be better off if he or she were not around. The AACAP says that teens who are considering suicide might "give verbal hints with statements such as: 'I won't be a problem for you much longer,' 'Nothing matters,' 'It's no use,' and 'I won't see you again.'"[7] Such remarks may be disregarded as nothing more than normal teenage angst and moodiness—an assumption that could prove to be not only erroneous, but deadly.

One teenage girl from Carol Stream, Illinois, had every intention of committing suicide before her parents found out and got her into treatment. The girl's personality had noticeably changed, and she exhibited nearly all the AACAP's warning signs. Formerly bubbly, chatty, and outgoing, she began to isolate herself from friends and family, heading straight to her room when she got home from school and spending hours at a time on Facebook. She seemed perpetually irritated, screaming at her little sister and arguing with her parents. She no longer even resembled the happy, active girl she once was. "I didn't want to talk to anyone anymore," she says. "I was uninterested."[8]

Why Do Teenagers Take Their Own Lives?

Whenever a young person has committed suicide, friends and family members invariably feel lost in shock and grief. Guilt is a typical emotion, with loved ones agonizing over why it happened and what they might have done to prevent it. Jim Wellborn, who is a child and adolescent psychologist from Brentwood, Tennessee, says the question of why teens would reach the point of wanting to die is mystifying. "There is no simple answer," he writes. "Even when you think you know the answer, it is likely to be only a partial truth."[9]

The reasons teens commit suicide can vary widely, but certain circumstances may serve as triggers in their decision to do so. Perhaps they are traumatized by a major disappointment or sense of failure, feel brokenhearted over a breakup with a boyfriend or girlfriend, or are despondent because of turmoil in their families. According to Wellborn, the problems facing teens can seem both overwhelming and insurmountable. "Without the perspective that comes from living for decades (rather than just years)," he writes, "even common problems can seem catastrophic

> " One condition that is closely associated with suicidal thoughts and behavior is depression. "

and permanent to young people. When this inexperience with life combines with real life difficulties, some kids can't see how things can ever get better." Faced with what they perceive to be never-ending despair, these troubled teens view dying as their only option. As Wellborn explains: "Suicide is seen as a way to get out from under the pain."[10]

Dangerous Depression

One condition that is closely associated with suicidal thoughts and behavior is depression. A severe mental illness that affects millions of people, depression causes sufferers to feel an overall sense of sadness and despair. It is much more common among teens than many people realize and is a leading contributor to teen suicide. Leading child and adolescent psychiatrist Harold Koplewicz writes: "We often hear that suicide is the third leading cause of death—after accidents and homicide—among teens and young adults between 15 and 24 years of age. What we don't often hear is that over 90 percent of all young people who commit suicide are suffering from severe mental illness. Depression is the leading condition in the suicides of adolescent boys and girls."[11]

Michael Blosil, the 18-year-old son of singer/entertainer Marie Osmond, suffered from depression for years and had spent time in a residential mental health facility. On February 26, 2010, Blosil committed suicide by jumping from the fifteenth-floor balcony of his Los Angeles apartment. In spite of his long-term battle with depression, he appeared to be happy and in good spirits, so his friends and family thought he was doing exceptionally well. Thus, his suicide was a complete shock, as his roommate Sean Srnik explains: "He was so jolly all the time. He's probably the funniest, happiest guy I've ever met in my life. It's something I would never expect from somebody like him."[12] In a suicide note that he left for his closest friend, Ruthann Clawson, Blosil said that he had taken his own life because he wanted to be at peace.

Substance Abuse and Teen Suicide

Just as depression has a strong connection with suicide, the same is true of drug and alcohol abuse. Studies have shown that teens who have substance abuse problems have a much higher risk of attempting suicide than those who do not use drugs or alcohol. According to the Substance Abuse and Mental Health Services Administration, evidence strongly supports the premise that abuse of alcohol and drugs is second only to mental disorders such as depression as a suicidal risk factor. Stan Kid, who is a lieutenant with the Malverne Police Department in Long Island,

New York, shares his thoughts about how the risk of suicide escalates when teens get drunk or high on drugs: "Nobody thinks clearly when they're flying."[13]

The causative link between substance abuse and teen suicide was shown in a study that was presented at the 2010 meeting of the American Psychiatric Association. The psychiatrists who performed the study analyzed the medical investigation records of 234 youth from North Carolina who had committed suicide between 1999 and 2008. They found that more than 51 percent had a history of mental illness and/or substance abuse, with 4.3 percent suffering from both conditions and 6.4 percent from substance abuse only. Another finding was that 11.5 percent of the youth had been intoxicated at the time of suicide. In their research abstract, the study's authors explain that the diagnosis of mental illness and substance abuse "is present in more than 50% of child/adolescent suicides, an important risk factor for suicide in child and adolescent populations for all races and both genders."[14]

> **Studies have shown that teens who have substance abuse problems have a much higher risk of attempting suicide than those who do not use drugs or alcohol.**

Is Suicide Contagious?

By their very nature, teenagers tend to be impressionable as well as impulsive. They are often influenced by the words and actions of other young people, particularly their friends. Mental health professionals say that vulnerable teens may be influenced to commit suicide after hearing about other teenagers who have done so. This is especially true when a suicide garners widespread publicity and young people perceive the death as being romanticized by the media.

An example of this "copycat effect" is a suicide cluster, a relatively rare occurrence in which a group of teens kill themselves in similar ways, usually over a period of weeks or months. Steve Gerali, who is a psychologist, youth pastor, and the author of *What Do I Do When Teenagers Are Depressed and Consider Suicide?*, explains: "Cluster suicide is a phenom-

Protesters demand stronger anti-bullying laws in New Jersey in 2010. Legislative hearings on those laws began after the suicide of an 18-year-old college student whose roommate broadcast intimate scenes between him and another man online. Cyberbullying has been implicated in a number of teen suicides.

enon that occurs when a teenager in a community or in a school commits suicide, and then all of a sudden there is an epidemic of attempts—and maybe completed—suicide."[15]

The city of Palo Alto, California, was the scene of a suicide cluster between May 2009 and January 2010. Five teenagers, including 2 females aged 13 and 17, and 3 males 16, 17, and 19, killed themselves in the exact same way—by throwing themselves in front of a speeding commuter train. According to Palo Alto police, at least 6 other teens were stopped before they could commit suicide at the same rail crossing. One was a 17-year-old boy who had walked to the tracks on the evening of

June 4, 2009. Noticing that he had been acting strangely at home, the teen's mother followed him and was terrified to see him standing in the middle of the tracks. She pleaded with him to get off, and with the help of a passing motorist, she was able to pull the young man to safety before he could be struck and killed by the train.

Does Bullying Drive Teenagers to Suicide?

Because of the worldwide reach of the Internet, along with television news and print media, bullying has received a vast amount of attention in recent years. Tragically, much of this publicity has resulted from teenagers who committed suicide after being bullied, both in person and through online social networking sites, instant messaging, e-mails, and cell phone text messaging. Some names have become known to millions of people, such as Phoebe Prince, Jessica Logan, Billy Lucas, Asher Brown, and Tyler Clementi—all teenagers who killed themselves in the wake of ridicule, viciousness, and cruel treatment by their peers. Psychologist Phil McGraw, who hosts the *Dr. Phil* daytime television show, writes: "Too many of these children become so distraught that they turn to desperate measures and do the unthinkable."[16]

No one could disagree that these and other teen suicides were senseless and tragic. And perhaps the teens would not have taken their own lives if they had not been bullied. Yet no one knows that for sure, just as no one can say with any certainty how much of a role bullying actually played in their decision to kill themselves. Were these teens really "bullied to death" as many claim? Or were they experiencing other problems, with bullying being one of many potential triggers? Paul Butler, an associate dean and professor of law at George Washington University, offers his opinion about the issue: "Suicide is a tragic response to bullying. It is also a rare response. Of the

> " With suicide a major cause of death for teenagers, mental health professionals, educators, parents, and other concerned groups overwhelmingly agree that this issue is urgent and must be treated as a priority. "

millions of children who suffer bullying, few take their own lives. Bullies 'cause' suicides in the same way that a man 'causes' the suicide of a lover he spurns."[17]

Can Teenage Suicide Be Stopped?

With suicide a major cause of death for teenagers, mental health professionals, educators, parents, and other concerned groups overwhelmingly agree that this issue is urgent and must be treated as a priority. The key is prevention—getting to kids long before they reach the point of attempting suicide. One widely supported step is engaging teens in a dialogue so they know people care about their feelings and are willing to help them. Treating suicide like a taboo subject that should not be discussed (as it often is) does nothing to help kids deal with complicated emotions, fears, and grief.

According to the National Alliance on Mental Illness, one of the most common misconceptions about talking with teenagers who may be suicidal is that bringing up the subject might push them toward committing suicide. "This is not true," the group writes. "There is no danger of 'giving someone the idea.' Rather, the opposite is correct."[18] The alliance states that discussing suicide openly and honestly, without displaying shock or disapproval, is one of the most important things parents and educators can do for teens.

A crucial component in preventing teen suicide is for psychological issues to be identified. Studies have consistently shown that depression, substance abuse, and/or other mental health disorders are at the root of nearly all suicidal thoughts and attempts. If these problems are addressed, many teen suicides could potentially be prevented. The National Alliance on Mental Illness explains: "The feelings that often lead to suicide are highly treatable. That's why it is imperative that we better understand the symptoms of the disorders and the behaviors that often accompany thoughts of suicide. With more knowledge, we can often prevent the devastation of losing a loved one."[19]

How Serious a Problem Is Teenage Suicide?

66 Suicide is an important public health problem in many countries, and is a leading cause of death amongst teenagers and young adults. 99

> —American Foundation for Suicide Prevention, which is dedicated to reducing loss of life from suicide.

66 Many youth believe that suicide is somehow romantic or heroic. They may fail to comprehend that death is irreversible and perceive death like a peaceful sleep that will make everything better. 99

> —R.J. Fetsch and C.L. Collins, Department of Human Development and Family Studies at Colorado State University, and D. Whitney, certified school counselor.

I t is a sobering reality that more than 16,000 teenagers die every year in the United States, and nearly three-fourths of those deaths are the result of unnatural causes—meaning they could have been prevented. The number one teen killer is accidental injuries (primarily motor vehicle crashes), which annually claim the lives of nearly 8,000 youth aged 12 to 19. Homicide is the second-most common cause of death for teenagers. Many people are not surprised by these statistics because they are widely publicized by groups such as the Centers for Disease Control and Prevention (CDC) and the National Highway Transportation Safety Administration. What is *not* so well known is that an estimated 1,841 teenagers die each year by killing themselves.

Parents in the Dark

With news about bullying and teen suicides being widely publicized over the last few years, the public is becoming more aware that vulnerable teenagers are at risk for taking their own lives. Yet the very idea that so many young people could reach the point where they no longer want to live seems not only tragic, but unbelievable. As the American Academy of Child & Adolescent Psychiatry writes: "That a teenager could be so unbearably unhappy that he would choose to kill himself is something that's almost too painful for a parent to examine. But with the increasing prevalence of teen suicide, no parent can afford to ignore the possibility."[20]

Even with the increased media coverage of teen suicide, parents are often not aware of how serious the problem is. This became apparent in a study that was published in the January 2010 issue of the journal *Pediatrics*. Parents who participated in a series of focus groups said that they considered suicide a major problem among teenagers—but only in other communities, not in their own. Kimberly A. Schwartz, one of the authors of the study, explains: "The thinking was that it might happen over there, but it doesn't happen to us."[21] Schwartz and her fellow researchers emphasize that suicide must be viewed as a potential problem in all communities because teens *everywhere* are at risk.

Teens Who Wish to Die

As shocking as it is that more than 1,800 young people take their own lives each year, suicides are far surpassed by the vast number of teenagers whose suicide attempt fails. The CDC explains: "Deaths from youth suicide are only part of the problem. More young people survive suicide attempts than actually die."[22] The CDC estimates that for every completed suicide by teens, there are 10 to 20 times as many suicide attempts. Yet because health officials have no way of knowing how many suicide attempts are reported as accidents—or not reported at all—the actual number of attempted suicides is likely larger than what is estimated.

The potential of teenagers being at risk for suicide was brought to light in a comprehensive study conducted by the CDC between September 2008 and December 2009. Known as the Youth Risk Behavior Survey, the study involved thousands of students in grades 9 through 12 at public and private schools throughout the United States. When asked questions about suicidal thinking and behavior, 13.8 percent of the teen participants said they had given serious thought to killing themselves. Even more disturbing was that nearly 11 percent of the teens said they had created a plan for how they would end their lives, and 6.3 percent had actually attempted suicide one or more times.

A Suicide Survivor

Josh Burnham was one of the teenagers who attempted suicide, and the fact that he survived was nothing short of miraculous. As an 18-year-old high school senior in suburban Philadelphia, Burnham seemed to be on top of the world. He had a loving relationship with his family and a happy home life. He was so popular in school that he had been voted onto the homecoming court, as well as being a star player on the varsity golf team and a standout baseball pitcher. His academic record was excellent, and he looked forward to college and an eventual career in broadcast journalism. Yet even with all that he had going for him, Burnham suffered from a deep, irrational fear that no matter what he did, it was not good enough. His parents knew he was troubled and had gotten him into counseling, but neither they nor his therapist had any idea how badly he was hurting. He never told anyone that he was thinking about killing himself to escape from the emotional pain.

On September 28, 2007, Burnham decided to end his life. He went to his bedroom, closed and barricaded the door, and called his girlfriend on the phone to say, "I'm sorry for letting you down. I have to go."[23] Then he crawled through his window onto the ninth-floor balcony and jumped, falling 90 feet (27.43m)

> " What is *not* so well known is that an estimated 1,841 teenagers die each year by killing themselves. "

and slamming into the ground below at an estimated 50 miles per hour (80.47kph). His body was battered, broken, and bloody—but when paramedics arrived to rush him to the hospital, they were astounded to find that he was still breathing.

For five days Burnham remained in a coma. A tracheotomy (throat incision) had been performed and a breathing tube inserted to keep him alive. His pelvis was crushed, his left leg was shattered, his wrist was broken, and his jaw was broken in four places. When he finally woke from the coma, he had no memory of what happened. He asked his sister who had pushed him out the window, and when she tearfully said that he was the only one in the room, he stared at her, stunned. He simply could not believe that he had tried to take his own life. "I never thought it would get to that point,"[24] he says.

> As shocking as it is that more than 1,800 young people take their own lives each year, suicides are far surpassed by the vast number of teenagers whose suicide attempt fails.

Convinced that he had been given a second chance for a reason, Burnham vowed to share his story with other young people. Now he travels to schools and shares his story with kids, talking to them about the problems that can lead to suicide. He lets them know that help is available and encourages them to stop and think before they make decisions that they can never take back. He writes: "I would never say I'm proud of what happened because that just sounds wrong. Why would you be proud of trying to commit suicide? I'm proud of taking a tragic situation that I did to myself and flipped it into something positive that I can talk about with confidence."[25]

Tragedy in a Welsh Community

Copycat suicides are a serious concern for health officials in cities and towns throughout the world. Many worry about the massive publicity that follows the suicide of one or more teenagers and its potential effect on vulnerable young people. Because teens are impressionable as well as impulsive, they may be influenced to follow the lead of others whose suicides they perceive to be romantic in some way. Madelyn S. Gould explains: "Many studies indicate that suicide contagion and imitation are real. The studies show increases in rates of completed suicides and attempts after news accounts of suicide."[26] According to Gould, media accounts that include excessively descriptive, lurid details about the teens involved, where suicides take place, and the methods used, can serve as a "how-to" guide for young people who identify with those who have killed themselves.

Nowhere has cluster suicide been a more tragic reality than in Bridgend County in Wales. Between January 2007 and February 2009, 24 young people hanged themselves and another killed himself by lying down in front of a moving train. Nearly all of the dead were teenagers, with a few in their twenties. The community was gripped with shock and fear, its residents having no idea what was causing these young people to want to die. Journalist Alex Shoumatoff traveled to Wales to investigate the suicides; he writes: "This isn't just a series of unrelated, individual acts. It's an outbreak—a localized epidemic—of a desire to leave this world that is particularly contagious to teenagers, who are impressionable and impulsive and, apparently in Bridgend, not finding many reasons for wanting to stick around."[27]

With the announcement of each new suicide in Bridgend County, the British media went wild. Front-page stories appeared with huge, blaring headlines such as "Another Girl Hangs Herself in Death Town," and "The Internet Suicide Cult?" Tabloid newspapers pronounced Bridgend to be "Britain's Bleakest Town," "Suicide Town," "Death Valley," and "Death-Cult Town." Before long the suicide cluster captured international attention, with news crews descending on the Welsh community from Germany, Spain, and the United States, among other countries. And the stories exemplified sensationalism, with explicit details about the suicides and large, color photos of the dead teens splashed across the front pages of newspapers day after day.

> " **Nowhere has cluster suicide been a more tragic reality than in Bridgend County in Wales.** "

The people of Bridgend County were furious, attacking the media for its insensitivity and holding it accountable for suicides that followed publication of the stories. Professionals who specialize in studying suicide clusters were disturbed as well as shocked by the media accounts of the deaths. Lars Johansson, who is with the Department of Community Medicine and Rehabilitation at Sweden's Umeå University, explains:

I was surprised about the publishing of the names and pictures of the victims and the surviving family. I do think that the media coverage in such detail contributed to the formation of this cluster. Teenagers are impulsive, and most suicide clusters described have concerned the young, including young adults. . . . What struck me was that many suicides appeared to have taken place in "public"—they did not hide away, they committed suicide by hanging themselves in public areas, as if they wanted to be found and noticed, "Look, here I am!"[28]

Alaskan Teens in Crisis

In the CDC's 2008 to 2009 youth risk study, information about teenagers was compiled for all U.S. states. The study found that high school students nationwide suffered from feelings of hopelessness and suicidal thoughts, and each state was touched by the tragedy of teen suicide. Other studies have also examined the problem in depth. What this research has revealed is that some states have a much higher rate of teen suicide than others—and Alaska has the most serious problem of all.

> **What this research has revealed is that some states have a much higher rate of teen suicide than others—and Alaska has the most serious problem of all.**

A May 2010 CDC report stated that each year from 1999 to 2006, the U.S. youth mortality rate averaged 49.5 deaths per 100,000 teens. Of those, 11 percent were suicides, meaning that an estimated 5.4 out of every 100,000 teens kill themselves annually. On the state level, statistics are much grimmer in Alaska. According to a January 2010 report by the Alaska Division of Public Health, 38 out of 100,000 teens committed suicide each year between 2005 and 2007. Although this is a significant improvement over 2003 to 2005, when 53 out of 100,000 teens killed themselves, it is still more than 7 times the national average.

An October 2010 story by an Alaskan news station referred to the state's high teen suicide rate as a tragic problem. The article referenced a conference of state leaders who had gathered to discuss the issue and to brainstorm about what measures could be taken to stop the crisis. In speaking about 11 teen suicides that had recently taken place during a six-week period, U.S. senator Lisa Murkowski of Alaska asked: "How are we failing our young people and what more can be done?"[29] Many parents attended the meeting, as did about a dozen teenagers. One girl spoke about the struggles that young people face and how painful it is for them when they see kids their own age killing themselves. She encouraged the community members to reach out to troubled teens, showing that they care and are willing to listen and help.

Teens in Distress

Of the 16,375 teenagers who die each year, more than 1,800 take their own lives. That may seem like a rather small number when compared with the thousands of teens who die in motor vehicle crashes, from other accidental injuries, or by homicide. But the deaths are especially tragic because they represent a group of kids who were suffering from such unbearable despair that they saw suicide as the only way out.

How Serious a Problem Is Teenage Suicide?

66 For over a century, suicide rates rose regularly with age and were highest amongst the elderly. Since the 1970s, this has no longer been the case in most Western countries, where suicide rates for young people have risen sharply, whilst the rate for old people has fallen steeply. 99

—Christian Baudelot and Roger Establet, *Suicide: The Hidden Side of Modernity*. Cambridge: Polity, 2008.

Baudelot and Establet are sociologists from France.

66 There's definitely been a noticeable increase in the rate of suicide among youth. In fact, some of the best data suggests that over the last 25 or 30 years the rate has nearly doubled among young people. 99

—Thomas Joiner, "Wise Counsel Interview Transcript: An Interview with Thomas Joiner, Ph.D. on Why People Commit Suicide," Mental Help Net, April 13, 2009. www.mentalhelp.net.

Joiner is a professor at Florida State University's Department of Psychology.

* Editor's Note: While the definition of a primary source can be narrowly or broadly defined, for the purposes of Compact Research, a primary source consists of: 1) results of original research presented by an organization or researcher; 2) eyewitness accounts of events, personal experience, or work experience; 3) first-person editorials offering pundits' opinions; 4) government officials presenting political plans and/or policies; 5) representatives of organizations presenting testimony or policy.

66 **Although rates of suicide and suicide attempts among teens and young adults remain distressingly high, the good news is that suicide rates for some adolescents appear to have gone down in the past few years.** 99

—Madelyn S. Gould, "Growing Pains: Adolescent Suicide Rates Raise Concerns," interviewed by HealthyPlace, March 17, 2010. www.healthyplace.com.

Gould is a professor of clinical psychiatry at Columbia University's College of Physicians and Surgeons.

66 **The figures for suicide do not include attempted suicide, which is up to 20 times more frequent than completed suicide.** 99

—John Henden, *Preventing Suicide: The Solution Focused Approach*. West Sussex, England: Wiley, 2009.

Henden is a psychologist from the United Kingdom.

66 **Those who attempt suicide and survive may have serious injuries like broken bones, brain damage, or organ failure.** 99

—Centers for Disease Control and Prevention, *Understanding Suicide Fact Sheet*, 2010. www.cdc.gov.

The CDC seeks to promote health and quality of life by controlling disease, injury, and disability.

66 **Suicides among young people continue to be a serious problem. Each year in the U.S., thousands of teenagers commit suicide.** 99

—American Academy of Child & Adolescent Psychiatry, "Teen Suicide," *Facts for Families*, May 2008. http://aacap.org.

The American Academy of Child & Adolescent Psychiatry's physician members research, evaluate, diagnose, and treat psychiatric disorders in children and adolescents.

66 **Wishing both to die and to live is typical of most individuals who are suicidal, even those who are seriously suicidal.** 99

—Substance Abuse and Mental Health Services Administration, *Addressing Suicidal Thoughts and Behaviors in Substance Abuse Treatment*, 2009. http://kap.samhsa.gov.

The Substance Abuse and Mental Health Services Administration is dedicated to reducing the impact of substance abuse and mental illness on America's communities.

66 **Historically, black teens and young adults have lower suicide rates than white teens, but in recent decades, the suicide rate for black youth has increased dramatically.** 99

—National Institute of Mental Health, "Black Teens, Especially Girls, at High Risk for Suicide Attempts," April 10, 2009. www.nimh.nih.gov.

An agency of the U.S. government, the National Institute of Mental Health is the largest scientific organization in the world specializing in mental illness research and the promotion of mental health.

How Serious a Problem
Is Teenage Suicide?

- According to a study published in the February 2010 issue of *Pediatrics*, **1,771 children and teens** between the ages of 10 and 19 committed suicide in the United States in 2006.

- From 1950 to 1990, the suicide rate for teens 15 to 19 years old increased by **300 percent**, then from 1990 to 2003, the rate in this age group decreased by **35 percent**.

- The National Institute of Mental Health states that in 2007, **5 times** as many males as females aged 15 to 19 died by suicide.

- A 2008 report by researchers from the United Kingdom showed that suicide rates among British youth aged 10 to 19 declined by **28 percent** from 1997 to 2003.

- The rate of suicide for Native American teens is **70 percent** higher than for youth of any other ethnic group in the United States.

- The Alaska Division of Public Health reports that the suicide rate for Alaska native teens is more than **8 times** higher than for Alaskan non-native teens.

- According to the National Center for Injury Prevention and Control, **683 children and teens** under the age of 19 committed suicide with guns in 2007.

Suicide Is the Third Leading Killer of Teens

According to a May 2010 CDC report, the top 3 causes of death for young people aged 12 to 19 are unintentional injuries (most often from motor vehicle crashes), homicide, and suicide. This chart shows the percent distribution of all teenage deaths from 1999 to 2006.

Leading causes of death for teenagers 12 to 19 years old

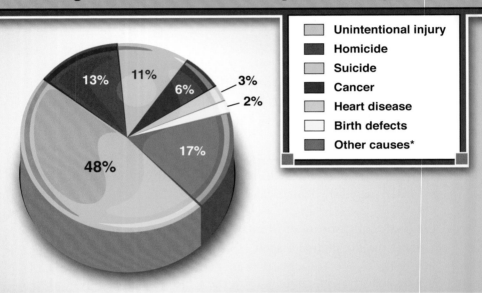

Legend:
- Unintentional injury
- Homicide
- Suicide
- Cancer
- Heart disease
- Birth defects
- Other causes*

*Other causes include chronic respiratory disease, influenza and pneumonia, other infectious diseases, stroke, and other chronic conditions (each of which accounts for less than 1 percent of all deaths).

Source: Arialdi M. Miniño, "Mortality Among Teenagers Aged 12–19 Years: United States, 1999–2006", *NCHS Data Brief*, May 2010. www.cdc.gov.

- The U.S. Department of Health and Human Services states that between 1970 and 1990, the suicide rate for youth aged 15 through 19 nearly doubled, from **5.9 to 11.1** per 100,000.

Suicide Methods

Teenagers use various methods to take their own lives. For females the most prevalent method is suffocation (usually hanging), whereas males typically use firearms. These and other suicide methods used by teens are illustrated on the graph below.

Percent of Suicides for Teens and Young Adults Aged 10 to 24 by Gender and Method, 2002–2006

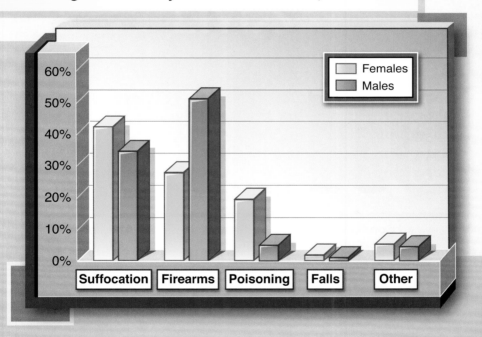

Source: Centers for Disease Control and Prevention, "National Suicide Statistics at a Glance," September 30, 2009. www.cdc.gov.

- According to the Centers for Disease Control and Prevention, the top three methods used in suicides of young people include firearms (**46 percent**), suffocation (**39 percent**), and poisoning (**8 percent**).

- The American Association of Suicidology states that since 1950, the suicide rate for males 15 to 24 years old has **quadrupled**, and for females it has **doubled**.

closely connected with teen suicide. The practice of inhaling the fumes of volatile solvents is commonly called huffing. These substances include commercial "canned air" spray for cleaning computer keyboards; glues, paints, paint thinner, and degreasing agents; air freshener and other products that come in aerosol cans; and fuels like gasoline, propane, and butane. Kids inhale the vapors of these substances to get a quick and cheap high—and by doing so, they run the risk of causing severe damage to their vital organs, as well as becoming suicidal.

> **Kids inhale the vapors of these substances to get a quick and cheap high—and by doing so, they run the risk of causing severe damage to their vital organs, as well as becoming suicidal.**

The connection between inhalant use and suicide has been examined in a number of studies conducted over the years. One of the studies, which was published in September 2007, involved 723 incarcerated teenagers. The researchers found that more than one-third of the teen participants had inhaled volatile substances in an attempt to get high—and the rate of suicidal attempts among those teens was shocking. The study showed that over 81 percent of the girls and 59.5 percent of the boys who had abused or were dependent on inhalants had attempted suicide. The University of Denver Graduate School of Social Work provides this synopsis: "The investigators found a remarkable increase in suicidal thoughts and attempts with higher levels of use of volatile solvents. In fact, the majority of those in the sample who had been serious abusers prior to incarceration reported having tried to kill themselves at some point."[37]

The researchers who performed the study acknowledge that the reasons for the link between inhalant use and suicidal thoughts and behavior are unknown. They also say that because all the teens in the study were incarcerated, some might question whether the findings apply to all youth. But they are convinced that there is overwhelming evidence to show the strong connection between huffing and suicide. They write:

It is notable that studies using community or school-based samples of adolescents have consistently demonstrated a relationship between inhalant use and suicidal thoughts . . . or suicide attempts. . . . The consistent relationship of inhalant use and suicidality, regardless of setting, suggests that the relationship between solvents and suicidality is not unique to incarcerated youth.[38]

"To End the Pain of Living"

Teenagers who reach the point where they view suicide as the only way out are suffering from emotional pain that many people cannot begin to understand. Sometimes their sadness and despair is obvious to their families and friends, but this is not always the case—as shown by the suicide of Alexis Pilkington. They may suffer from depression, bipolar disorder, substance abuse, or other mental health disorders, but whatever their problems, the sense of despair they feel is deep, intense, and overwhelming. Often the loved ones they leave behind are filled with unbearable shock and grief, wondering whether they could have done something to prevent the suicide. As the Youth Suicide Prevention Program writes: "We don't know for sure because when youth die by suicide they take the answers with them. But teens who attempt suicide and survive tell us that they wanted to die to end the pain of living."[39]

Primary Source Quotes*

Why Do Teenagers Take Their Own Lives?

❝Since depression and related illnesses are the driving forces behind most suicides, it's easy to see why I call them potential killers.❞

—Gary E. Nelson, *A Relentless Hope: Surviving the Storm of Teen Depression*. Eugene, OR: Cascade, 2007.

Nelson is a minister and pastoral counselor who lives in Boaz, West Virginia.

❝Mental disorders constitute a clear risk factor for suicidal behavior.❞

—Thomas Joiner, *Myths About Suicide*. Cambridge, MA: Harvard University Press, 2010.

Joiner is a professor of psychology at Florida State University.

❝A family history of suicidal behavior greatly increases the risk in teens and young adults.❞

—Madelyn S. Gould, "Growing Pains: Adolescent Suicide Rates Raise Concerns," interviewed by HealthyPlace, March 17, 2010. www.healthyplace.com.

Gould is a professor of clinical psychiatry at Columbia University's College of Physicians and Surgeons.

* Editor's Note: While the definition of a primary source can be narrowly or broadly defined, for the purposes of Compact Research, a primary source consists of: 1) results of original research presented by an organization or researcher; 2) eyewitness accounts of events, personal experience, or work experience; 3) first-person editorials offering pundits' opinions; 4) government officials presenting political plans and/or policies; 5) representatives of organizations presenting testimony or policy.

❝It should be remembered that suicidal people experience unbearable pain, not always depression, and even if they do experience depression, the critical stimulus is the 'unbearable' nature of the depression.❞

—Frederick T.L. Leong and Mark M. Leach, eds., introduction to *Suicide Among Racial and Ethnic Minority Groups*. New York: Routledge, 2008.

Leong is a professor of psychology at Michigan State University, and Leach is the director of training in the Department of Psychology at the University of Southern Mississippi.

❝Depression is too often interpreted as teen petulance and ignored. Changes in behavior are similarly written off as a kid just being a kid and going through a phase.❞

—Stan Kid, e-mail interview with author, October 11, 2010.

Kid is a lieutenant with the Malverne Police Department in Long Island, New York.

❝Recognize that adolescent angst is part of normal development, but adolescent depression is not; it's a very real illness that, left untreated, is potentially lethal.❞

—Harold Koplewicz, "Suicide and the Antidepressant Question," *Huffington Post*, March 9, 2010. www.huffingtonpost.com.

Koplewicz is a nationally known child and adolescent psychiatrist from New York.

❝Each year, thousands of at-risk teens are diagnosed with clinical depression. . . . If left untreated or ignored, it can be a devastating illness for the teen and their family and it can lead to suicide.❞

—Mark Gregston, "Teen Suicide Facts You Need to Know," *Christian Post*, July 17, 2010. www.christianpost.com.

Gregston is the founder and executive director of Heartlight, a residential counseling program for struggling adolescents.

❝In the presence of depression and other risk factors, ready access to guns and other weapons, medications or other methods of self-harm increases suicide risk.❞

—American Foundation for Suicide Prevention, "When You Fear Someone May Take Their Life," 2010. www.afsp.org.

The American Foundation for Suicide Prevention is dedicated to reducing loss of life from suicide.

....

❝The first thing about suicide that I like people to know is that some form of depression is almost always present in the suicidal person.❞

—Bev Cobain, interviewed by Brian Libby, "Even in His Youth," CVS Health Resources, April 28, 2009. www.cvshealthresources.com.

Cobain is a psychiatric nurse whose cousin, Nirvana lead singer Kurt Cobain, shot himself to death in 1994.

....

❝Combine a teen's emotional turmoil with getting into drugs and/or alcohol, and you have a seriously potent combination.❞

—John M. Grohol, "Suicide, Celebrity and Young Adulthood," Psych Central, March 1, 2010. http://psychcentral.com.

Grohol is a psychologist and founder of the Psych Central website.

....

Why Do Teenagers Take Their Own Lives?

- The National Youth Violence Prevention Resource Center says that more than **90 percent** of teens who kill themselves suffer from a mental disorder such as depression or substance abuse.

- According to the American Psychiatric Association, depression increases the risk of a first suicide attempt by at least **14-fold**.

- The American Psychiatric Association states that more than **50 percent** of young people who commit suicide were substance abusers.

- According to a 2009 paper by the Substance Abuse and Mental Health Services Administration, emergency departments nationwide handled over 15,000 drug-related suicide attempts by youth aged 12 to 17 in 2004, and nearly **75 percent** were serious enough to warrant hospitalization.

- Clinical psychologist Wendy Lader states that people who **intentionally injure themselves** are nine times more likely to attempt suicide than non-self-injurers.

- The American Academy of Pediatrics states that the risk of teen suicide is 4 to 10 times higher in **homes with guns** than in homes without.

- According to the National Youth Violence Prevention Resource Center, many teens who kill themselves have at least one close **family member** who attempted or committed suicide.

Teen Depression Leads to Suicide

Studies have shown a strong connection between depression and suicide. In fact, child and adolescent psychiatrist Dr. Harold Koplewicz says that untreated depression is the number-one cause of teen suicide.

◆◆◆ Warning signs of depression ◆◆◆

- **Frequent bouts of sadness, crying**
- **Decreased interest in activities, inability to enjoy previously favorite activities**
- **Hopelessness**
- **Persistent boredom, low energy**
- **Social isolation, poor communication**
- **Low self-esteem, guilt**
- **Extreme sensitivity to rejection or failure**
- **Increased irritability, anger, or hostility**
- **Difficulty with relationships**
- **Frequent complaints of physical illnesses such as headaches and stomachaches**
- **Poor concentration**
- **A major change in eating and/or sleeping patterns**
- **Thoughts or expressions of suicide or self-destructive behavior**
- **Frequent absences from or poor performance at school**
- **Talk of or efforts to run away from home**

Source: American Academy of Child and Adolescent Psychiatry, "The Depressed Child," *Facts for Families*, May 2008. www.aacap.org.

The Link Between Mental Illness, Substance Abuse, and Suicide

Studies have consistently shown that teens who commit suicide often suffer from serious mental health problems such as depression and substance abuse. This connection was confirmed in a study announced in 2010, which involved analyzing the medical records of 234 youth from North Carolina who committed suicide between 1999 and 2008. The researchers' findings are shown on the graph below.

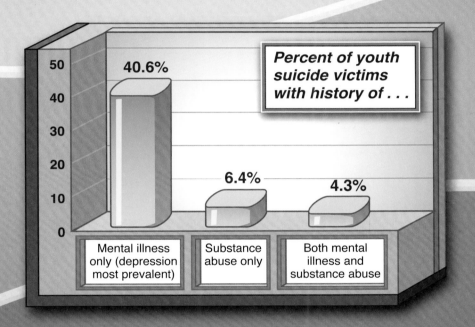

Percent of youth suicide victims with history of . . .

- Mental illness only (depression most prevalent): 40.6%
- Substance abuse only: 6.4%
- Both mental illness and substance abuse: 4.3%

Source: Yilmaz Yildirim, Ummuhan Yesil-Dagli, and Richard Bloch, "Prevalence of Mental Illness and Substance Abuse Among Child and Adolescent Suicide Victims," *New Research Abstracts to the 2010 Annual Meeting*, American Psychiatric Association, May 2010. www.psych.org.

- The National Youth Violence Prevention Resource Center states that teens are more likely to kill themselves if they have recently **read, seen, or heard about** other suicide attempts.

High Suicide Rates for Alaska Native Teens

According to a 2010 report by the Alaska Division of Public Health, from 1996 to 2005 the suicide rate for teens from Alaska's indigenous populations was more than 8 times higher than for nonnative teens. Health officials attribute this to the disproportionately high number of native youth who suffer from depression, anxiety, and substance abuse, along with inadequate access to mental health services. This graph shows the rate of suicides among indigenous Alaskan teens compared with nonnative teens.

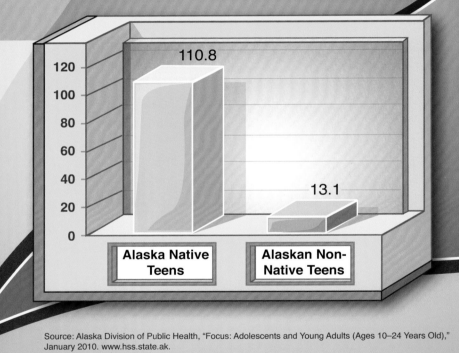

Suicides–Alaska Native vs. nonnative teens, 1996 to 2005 (per 100,000 teen population)

Source: Alaska Division of Public Health, "Focus: Adolescents and Young Adults (Ages 10–24 Years Old)," January 2010. www.hss.state.ak.

- According to the Substance Abuse and Mental Health Services Administration, individuals treated for alcohol abuse or dependence are at about **10 times** greater risk to eventually die by suicide compared with the general population.

Does Bullying Drive Teenagers to Suicide?

> "Bullying can worsen the mental health of teenagers who are already dealing with stress—and adolescents who experience teen bullying are more likely to report thoughts of suicide and suicidal behavior."
>
> —Mayo Clinic, a world-renowned medical facility headquartered in Rochester, Minnesota.

> "Another teenager killed himself because of bullying and anti-gay harassment. . . . School officials, wary of conservative protests, did nothing."
>
> —Jim David, writer for television and for the gay and lesbian newsmagazine the *Advocate*.

Numerous studies have shown that bullying is a serious problem among children and adolescents. That is true whether it involves physical pushing and shoving, verbal harassment, making fun of someone's disabilities or sexual orientation, or spewing abusive remarks on a computer screen. No matter how it is done, bullying can cause immense pain and suffering for anyone on the receiving end. Some young people reach the point of feeling so heartbroken, so beaten down, that they would rather die than cope with being bullied even one more day. As police lieutenant Stan Kid writes: "Kids haven't yet developed the psychological armor to deal with that kind of intellectual warfare and too often see suicide as the only way out."[40]

Driven to Desperation

Tragically, 16-year-old Alex Harrison was one of those teens. After enduring brutal bullying by a group of popular kids at his school in Cadillac, Michigan, he became so distraught that he saw suicide as his only escape. A quiet, highly intelligent teen who was known for his sense of humor, Alex had long been the victim of bullying by this group. They harassed and taunted him day after day, surrounding him in a secluded hallway when no one else was around, chanting "Creeper, Creeper" over and over again. As much as this hurt Alex, he never told his parents how bad the bullying was. Instead, he kept it to himself.

The last incident took place on February 6, 2009. Students who witnessed it said that Alex walked by a table in the cafeteria where some kids from the group were sitting. They began their usual taunting, calling him names, telling him to get away from them. Alex stopped and looked at one of the girls who was considered a leader of the group. She sneered at him, asking whether he knew that everyone hated him and did not want him around anymore.

> **Some young people reach the point of feeling so heartbroken, so beaten down, that they would rather die than cope with being bullied even one more day.**

That night, after Alex's parents returned home from a movie, they talked a while before going to bed. Alex's father, Tom Harrison, says that they planned to go skeet shooting early the next morning, so he reminded Alex not to stay up too late. "I told him, 'I love you Al,'" Tom says. "And that was the last time I ever spoke to my son."[41]

Before dawn, Alex left the house, walked far out into the woods, and shot himself to death. When Tom Harrison discovered his son's body, he found a note that Alex had written: "I am nothing. Sure it will get better but all of life isn't as it appears. I want to see if the God I believe in is real, and I'm not waiting 80 plus years for that. I love you guys. Alex." Perhaps as an afterthought, Alex added these words at the end of the note: "No funeral, no bullshit, if I am still alive after this is read, kill me please."[42]

A Serious, Pervasive Problem

Whether bullying is more prevalent today than in years past is unknown. What *is* known is that it is rampant most everywhere kids congregate, be it in school classrooms, cafeterias, and hallways; gymnasiums and athletic fields; or virtual gathering places such as Facebook and MySpace. Coree Davis, a high school senior who has been the victim of bullying since he was in elementary school, shares his thoughts: "You try to just tell yourself it's fine. Just let them do what they do, and you will do what you do, and try your best to be happy. Then it keeps re-occurring, and you can't take it anymore."[43]

The widespread prevalence of bullying was revealed in a study published in 2009 by researchers from the National Institutes of Health. After analyzing surveys completed by more than 7,000 adolescents, the team could clearly see that bullying was a serious problem for thousands of young people. Nearly 21 percent of the teens reported being physically bullied in the past 2 months, and 53.6 percent had been verbally harassed. More than half had experienced bullying in social situations, and 13.6 percent had been cyberbullied.

The latter category, cyberbullying, has taken bullying to a whole new level—and it is a problem that many health officials, educators, and parents say is growing worse. The Internet makes it easy for bullies to hurt their victims deeply, and in some cases completely destroy their reputations. Scott Hirschfeld, who is with the Anti-Defamation League's education division, explains: "Even if you turn off your computer you know that web page is up, or that people are spreading this rumor about you. The relentlessness of it is very psychologically devastating."[44]

Cyber Viciousness

Online social networking sites and cell phone text messaging provide teens with an unprecedented ability to abuse their peers by spreading rumors, gossip, and lies quickly and widely. In the past, victims of bullying could escape from the abuse once they were away from school and at home, but that is not possible with electronic media. Like an insidious stalker, the abuse follows wherever they go. Psychologist Steve Gerali explains: "What happens is kids who are cyber-bullied tend to see this as a hopeless situation—no matter where they go, they can't escape it because it's online. So suicide becomes a means to escape it."[45]

Jessica Logan made that tragic choice at the age of 18. Pretty, vivacious, popular, and known as someone who always stood up for her friends, Logan made the mistake of engaging in a practice known as "sexting." Using her cell phone, she sent a nude photograph of herself to a boy she had been dating for a short time. After they broke up, he shared the photo with four teenage girls, who then forwarded it to others. By the time Logan found out that her photo had been passed on, hundreds of kids had seen it. This led to a smear campaign, with Logan being shunned and called vile names, both in person and online.

> **The Internet makes it easy for bullies to hurt their victims deeply, and in some cases completely destroy their reputations.**

The brutal harassment had a devastating effect on Logan. Her personality changed from bubbly and outgoing to depressed and withdrawn, and she spent a great deal of time crying. Her best friend, Lauren Taylor, says that Logan called her constantly, sobbing on the phone because of the abuse that seemed to follow her everywhere she went. Taylor explains:

> I'd be with her and she'd get numbers that weren't even in her contacts, random numbers that she didn't know, texting her, "You're a whore, you're a slut." Or, she'd get on MySpace and get messages from people calling her those names, or Facebook would be the same way. It was constant. She'd go home thinking, "Oh I'm going to get away from this," but she never could get away from it.[46]

Taylor was a good friend to Logan, as were many others. They tried to protect her somehow from the abuse, but they could not. The damage was done, and she was heartbroken. On July 3, 2008, Logan went into her bedroom and hanged herself from a clothing rod in her closet. Her mother cries when she describes finding her only child dead. "She snapped," she says. "It was just too much for an 18-year-old girl to go through."[47]

The "Bullycide" Debate

The role that bullying plays in teen suicide is a topic of controversy. No one disputes the fact that young people taking their own lives is tragic. The debate revolves around whether bullying can *cause* teens to kill themselves or rather is one of many possible contributing factors. In referring to the highly publicized suicides of teens who were victims of bullying, school security expert Ken Trump writes:

> I certainly do not question whether these kids were bullied. I do not question whether the bullying added significant stress to the lives of these kids and others who are chronically bullied. And I definitely do not minimize the seriousness of the losses of these innocent kids' lives. But I am also not convinced that bullying [by] itself is the sole cause of teens taking their own life. Being "bullied to death" makes quite a media headline and soundbite. But does it accurately reflect the sole cause of death implied by the use of such a phrase?[48]

Trump says that he can understand how bullying could be the "last straw" for teens who are troubled by mental health issues and how it could potentially push them over the edge. But he is convinced that the premise of bullycide, or teens being bullied to death, deflects attention from the deeper role of existing mental health problems. Bullying alone, he says, does not cause suicide.

> ❝ The role that bullying plays in teen suicide is a topic of controversy. ❞

Yet even though most teens who commit suicide suffer from depression or other mental health problems, this is not true for all. Alex Harrison was not depressed, nor did he use alcohol or drugs. His parents say that he was a happy, sensitive teen who had been beaten down by relentless bullying over an extended period of time. Finally, it got to him. Tom Harrison explains: "Was my son bullied to death? No one knows why someone takes their own life, only the person knows that. But yes, I definitely think that bullying was a causative factor in Alex's decision to take his own life. It had a cumulative effect to the point where he felt he couldn't take it anymore."[49]

The Cruelty of Intolerance

It is a sad reality that teens who are perceived as "different" in some way often become the targets of bullies, and that includes teens who are bullied because of their sexual orientation. A survey by the Gay, Lesbian and Straight Education Network found that about 90 percent of nonheterosexual teens in middle school and high school were bullied in 2009. According to psychiatrist Harold Koplewicz, gay and lesbian teens are four times more likely than straight teens to attempt suicide. He writes: "Over the past few weeks it has been impossible to miss the flood of news stories about gay teens ending their own lives after enduring anti-gay bullying. Eighteen-year-old Tyler Clementi, 15-year-old Billy Lucas, and 13-year-olds Asher Brown and Seth Walsh were living in different corners of America . . . but each of them was subjected to the same kind of intolerance and cruelty."[50]

> According to psychiatrist Harold Koplewicz, gay and lesbian teens are four times more likely than straight teens to attempt suicide.

Clementi was a freshman at Rutgers University. He was a quiet young man, a gifted violinist who was known for his intelligence and kindness. On September 19, 2010, he asked his roommate, Dharun Ravi, if he could have some privacy that evening. Ravi agreed—but unbeknownst to Clementi, Ravi had set up a webcam before he left their room. From a friend's room, Ravi then proceeded to film and broadcast intimate scenes of Clementi and a male guest via live streaming video on the web. At the same time, Ravi was posting voyeuristic commentary on Twitter: "Roommate asked for the room till midnight. I went into Molly's room and turned on my webcam. I saw him making out with a dude. Yay."[51]

When Clementi learned that not only had his privacy been violated, but also shared with an unknown number of other people, he was devastated. On September 22, 2010, sometime after 8:00 P.M., he used his cell phone to update his Facebook status with a chilling farewell message: "Jumping off the gw bridge sorry."[52] Then he drove to the George Washington Bridge, got out of his car, and leaped to his death.

Death by Despair

As painful as bullying can be for teens, most who are bullied do not resort to suicide. But for those who feel like they cannot take it anymore, suicide may seem like the only means of escape. This is what happened to Alex Harrison. In his memory, Harrison's parents now work to educate teens about the dangers of bullying in the hope that other young lives may be saved. His mother writes: "What's really tragic is that it goes on, in every single school, all over this nation. Our mission to honor Alex is to never never never have it happen again. Maybe a pipe dream, but one we chose to live by."[53]

Primary Source Quotes*

Does Bullying Drive Teenagers to Suicide?

66 **Many of us know from our childhood experiences that bullying has long-lasting consequences for targets. Studies have linked bullying to increased rates of childhood and adult depression, suicide, aggression, and lower academic achievement.** 99

—Stan Davis, *Schools Where Everyone Belongs: Practical Strategies for Reducing Bullying.* Champaign, IL: Research, 2007.

Davis is a social worker and school guidance counselor who founded the website Stop Bullying Now!

66 **When technology takes traditional bullying into cyberspace, the damage can be catastrophic.** 99

—Wendy Sachs, "New Poll Finds Bullying Is Parents' Greatest Fear: Goodbye Stranger Danger, Hello Facebook Friend," *Huffington Post*, October 19, 2010. www.huffingtonpost.com.

Sachs is a former television producer who is now editor in chief of the family support website Care.com.

* Editor's Note: While the definition of a primary source can be narrowly or broadly defined, for the purposes of Compact Research, a primary source consists of: 1) results of original research presented by an organization or researcher; 2) eyewitness accounts of events, personal experience, or work experience; 3) first-person editorials offering pundits' opinions; 4) government officials presenting political plans and/or policies; 5) representatives of organizations presenting testimony or policy.

was plagued by an irrational fear that her grades were not good enough.

The girl continued on this downhill slide, growing more and more depressed. One night after a fight with her mother, she stood in front of a mirror in her room, wrapped a scarf around her neck, and then watched her face turn blue as she pulled the scarf tighter. She began to think about people who commit suicide, and then wondered: "'Maybe I could do it too. I could be out of all this, and I wouldn't have to deal with it anymore. It would be done.'"[54]

Intervention That Saved a Life

The girl considered the incident sort of a dress rehearsal for the real thing, and she now knew she could go through with it when the time was right. She put down the scarf and signed on to Facebook, and seeing that a friend was online, she began an instant message chat. When the friend asked how she was doing, the girl answered that she was feeling really bad. The friend asked what was wrong, and the girl replied: "Oh, I'm basically planning to go commit suicide."[55] The friend tried to talk her out of it, telling her that lots of people cared about her, but the girl ignored the comments and signed off.

Rather than keeping the conversation to herself, the friend told a school counselor, who in turn told the girl's parents. At school the next day, she was called in to the guidance office, where a counselor, a psychologist, and her parents were waiting. "The young woman who reported it may have saved a life," says Paula Clayton, who is medical director of the American Foundation for Suicide Prevention. "It's an ideal outcome to a very serious situation."[56] The girl was placed in a therapy program, and because she was considered a high suicide risk, she spent several weeks in a crisis stabilization unit at an Illinois hospital.

> " Although some teens commit suicide without giving any warning ahead of time, most say or do things that warn of their intention to take their own lives. "

Although the girl went through a very difficult time during her recovery, she slowly began making progress. Therapy taught her how to recognize whether she is sliding back into depression, and if that happens she does not hesitate to tell someone. She no longer thinks about suicide and has a renewed outlook on life. She explains: "You have to find some kind of motivation to pull you out of it. Mine happens to be my future, my family, my friends, what I want to do. . . . It can be hard to find that motivation, but people have to push you. You have to find someone who cares enough about you to help you along, because you can't do it by yourself."[57]

When Warning Signs Are Ignored

Studies have shown that when teens threaten to kill themselves, they are often not taken seriously—and that is a mistake that can have tragic consequences. A teenager *might* just be going through a phase or want attention or be spouting off because it has been a bad week. Perhaps he or she would never actually dream of committing suicide. But if parents, educators, or friends hear such a threat, they must err on the side of caution and assume that the teen is 100 percent serious. The mental health website HealthyPlace explains: "No doubt you have heard that people who talk about suicide won't really do it. It isn't true. . . . Suicide threats and similar statements should always be taken seriously."[58]

> **Studies have shown that when teens threaten to kill themselves, they are often not taken seriously—and that is a mistake that can have tragic consequences.**

A teenage girl named Christy often talked about having suicidal thoughts, but no one but her best friend Mary (not her real name) took her seriously. Christy had been physically and emotionally abused by her parents, and on more than one occasion she had threatened suicide. Finally, Christy reached her breaking point. She felt that she could no longer cope with the pain and killed herself at the age of 15. Mary writes: "Kids get to that point for *so many* reasons. Some kids are crying out for help the only way they think they'll be heard, and some seriously want to end it. I truly believe that a parent can turn it around in a second. Or a teacher, or any adult who can step in and do something."[59]

Healing Depression

Because depression is common among suicidal teenagers, early diagnosis can potentially save lives. Depression is considered a highly treatable illness, and with the right treatment many teens have overcome it. But since the illness's symptoms are often mistaken for normal teenage angst, most teens are never diagnosed. Rich Lieberman, chair of the Emergency Assistance Team of the National Association of School Psychologists, explains: "Truly, depression is the silent epidemic in the schools today."[60]

When a teen is thought to be suffering from depression, professional counseling is usually the first recommendation. One type of therapy, known as cognitive behavioral therapy (CBT), has been shown to be effective in treating about 60 percent of depressed teens. The method is based on the premise that they can be taught to recognize and react to negative thoughts and stressors in a positive, appropriate manner. According to Anne Marie Albano, a CBT researcher from Columbia University, emotionally vulnerable young people sometimes develop a habit of viewing life through a dark filter. A December 9, 2008, HealthyPlace article explains: "For reasons not clear—in some cases

> **Because depression is common among suicidal teenagers, early diagnosis can potentially save lives.**

due to genetics, trauma or a combination of the two—these kids enter their teen years seeing themselves as helpless and inferior, and the world around them and their future as bleak."[61]

Unlike some types of psychotherapy, CBT does not focus on the reasons for this negative outlook on life. Rather, the goal is to help depressed teens learn that they are in control of it. Albano says the first step is to help them understand that their negative mood is rooted in their view of the world as a glass that is half-empty, rather than half-full. They likely have a habit of assuming that the worst possible outcome of a situation is the one they can expect to occur, or ignoring successes while focusing on failures and mistakes. Through CBT, teens learn that these attitudes can be changed over time with practice. As with traditional psychotherapy, says Albano, "some of the benefit comes simply by giving the feelings words, and by identifying what triggers them."[62]

All in the Family

Another type of therapy that has been successful focuses on the entire family, rather than solely on the teen. Known as attachment-based family therapy, it has proved to significantly reduce suicidal thoughts in young people. Guy S. Diamond, a psychologist who directs the Center for Family Intervention Science at the Children's Hospital of Philadelphia, explains:

> Most treatment models mainly work with the adolescents alone, helping them to learn new coping and problem solving strategies. But adolescents are highly influenced by their parents. Family conflict, chaos, and strife can contribute to youth suicide, while at the same time family love, trust, and communication can buffer against it. This therapy aims to resolve family conflicts and promote family strengths so that the appropriate bond of attachment can protect youth from self harm.[63]

In February 2010 Diamond and his colleagues announced a study that involved 66 youth between the ages of 12 and 17, all of whom had received medical attention for severe suicidal thinking. After participating in family-based therapy, the teens were found to be at least 4 times less likely to have any suicidal thoughts than young people who underwent traditional one-on-one psychotherapy. According to Diamond, parents are not viewed as the problem, but as the "curative medicine." He says that they are the key to keeping lines of communication open in order to be cognizant of suicidal thinking and behavior.

A Program Focused on Prevention

In an effort to address the hopelessness and despair that drives teens to suicide, schools throughout the United States are starting to implement suicide awareness and prevention programs. One program, known as Signs of Suicide, has been used in thousands of schools and has helped reduce the number of suicide attempts. As a result of its success, the program is listed on the National Registry of Effective Programs, which is maintained by the Substance Abuse and Mental Health Services Administration.

66 Some suicide attempts are carefully planned and others are not. Either way, it is important to understand that suicidal feelings and actions are symptoms of an illness that must be treated. 99

—National Institute of Mental Health, "How Does Bipolar Disorder Affect Children and Teens Differently than Adults?," September 9, 2010. www.nimh.nih.gov.

An agency of the U.S. government, the National Institute of Mental Health is the largest scientific organization in the world specializing in mental illness research and the promotion of mental health.

66 The good news is that research over the last several decades has uncovered a wealth of information on the causes of suicide and on prevention strategies. 99

—Centers for Disease Control and Prevention, "Youth Suicide," August 4, 2008. www.cdc.gov.

The Centers for Disease Control and Prevention seeks to promote health and quality of life by controlling disease, injury, and disability.

Can Teenage Suicide Be Prevented?

- According to Mental Health America, four out of five teens who attempt suicide have given **clear warnings** of their intentions.

- The Substance Abuse and Mental Health Services Administration states that only about **36 percent** of young people at risk for suicide receive treatment or counseling.

- According to the National Institute of Mental Health, a type of psychotherapy known as cognitive behavioral therapy has been shown to reduce the rate of repeated suicide attempts by **50 percent** during a year of follow-up.

- In a study published in the January 2010 issue of *Pediatrics*, researchers stated that only **2 percent** of teens who have attempted suicide receive medical attention.

- The National Institute of Mental Health states that a treatment known as **dialectical behavior therapy** has been shown to reduce suicide attempts by **50 percent** among people with borderline personality disorder, a serious disorder of emotion regulation.

- According to child and adolescent psychiatrist Harold Koplewicz, up to **80 percent** of teens who suffer from depression can be successfully treated if they seek help from a doctor or therapist.

SOS Saves Lives

Due to increasing awareness of the seriousness of teen suicide, many schools are implementing prevention programs for students. One, known as Signs of Suicide (SOS), has helped reduce the number of suicide attempts. The program involves guided classroom discussions and screening for signs of depression and suicide risk. One study of the SOS program involved 4,133 students from 9 high schools in Georgia, Massachusetts, and Connecticut. About half were involved in the SOS program, and the remainder served as the control group. Questionnaires completed by the students 3 months after program implementation showed lower rates of suicidal thoughts and behaviors among participants.

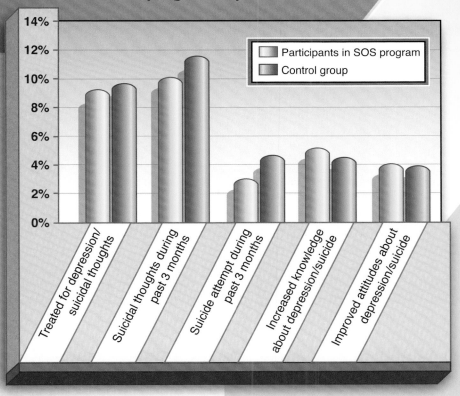

Signs of Suicide progress 3 months after program implementation

Source: Robert H. Aseltine Jr. et al., "Evaluating the SOS Suicide Program," *BMC Public Health*, July 18, 2007. www.ncbi.nlm.nih.gov.

Family Therapy Helps Suicidal Teens

Teens who suffer from depression and/or suicidal thoughts are often treated with therapy, and one type, known as attachment-based family therapy, has proven to help young people overcome these problems. This was evident in a study published in February 2010 involving 66 youth between the ages of 12 and 17, all of whom had received medical attention for severe suicidal thinking. After participating in the family-based therapy, the teens were found to be significantly less likely to have any suicidal thoughts than young people who underwent individual therapy.

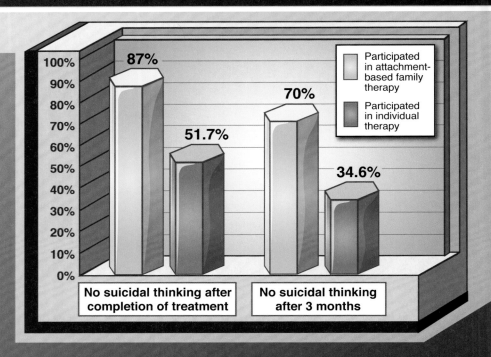

Source: Guy S. Diamond et al., "Attachment-Based Family Therapy for Adolescents with Suicidal Ideation: A Randomized Controlled Trial," *Department of Psychiatry and Human Behavior Faculty Papers,* 2010. http://jdc.jefferson.edu.

- A study published in the January 2010 issue of *Pediatrics* stated that suicide prevention efforts typically involve **environmental modification** such as restricting access to firearms, knives, or medications.

Prevention Efforts Have Mixed Results

Attempted suicides involving teenagers have remained fairly steady for nearly two decades (although 2007–2009 saw a slight decrease) while the number of teens experiencing suicidal thoughts has steadily declined during that same period. The declines might be influenced by increased awareness of teen suicide factors, widespread education, and prevention programs in schools and improved screening and treatment options for mental disorders such as depression.

Percentage of teenagers in grades 9–12 with suicidal thoughts and suicide attempts 1991 to 2009

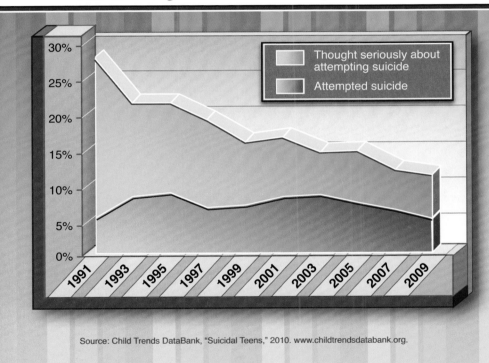

Source: Child Trends DataBank, "Suicidal Teens," 2010. www.childtrendsdatabank.org.

- A report published in 2007 showed that suicide attempts were reduced by **40 percent** for teens who participated in a prevention program called **Signs of Suicide**.

Key People and Advocacy Groups

American Association of Suicidology: An organization whose goal is to better understand and prevent suicide.

American Foundation for Suicide Prevention: A group that seeks to prevent suicide through research, education, and advocacy.

International Association for Suicide Prevention: An organization that seeks to prevent suicidal behavior and to provide a forum for academics, mental health professionals, crisis workers, and suicide survivors.

Megan Meier: A 13-year-old girl from Missouri who committed suicide after being repeatedly bullied by a neighbor woman posing as a teenage boy. Meier's death garnered national attention and public support for legislation to protect young people from bullying.

Mental Health America: A group that is dedicated to helping people live mentally healthier lives and to educating the public about mental health and mental illness.

National Alliance on Mental Illness: An organization that is dedicated to improving the lives of people who suffer from mental illness, as well as the lives of their families.

National Institute of Mental Health: An agency of the U.S. government and the largest scientific organization in the world specializing in mental illness research and the promotion of mental health.

Jane Pearson: A psychologist with the National Institute of Mental Health who is a leading expert on suicide.

Linda Sanchez: A U.S. representative from California who introduced the Megan Meier Cyberbullying Prevention Act, which would make it a federal crime to harass, intimidate, or cause substantial emotional stress to someone using electronic media.

Society for the Prevention of Teen Suicide: An advocacy organization that develops and implements youth suicide prevention programs at both the state and national level.

Suicide Prevention Action Network: A group that seeks to reduce loss of life from suicide by supporting research, educational campaigns, and policy initiatives.

Suicide Prevention Resource Center: A group that supports organizations and individuals in the development of suicide prevention programs, interventions, and policies.

Youth Suicide Prevention Program: An organization that seeks to end teen suicide by increasing the public's awareness of the problem and by educating families about risk factors and effective prevention measures.

Chronology

1952
The first edition of the American Psychiatric Association's *Diagnostic and Statistical Manual of Mental Disorders* is published, ushering in the formal classification of modern mental illnesses.

1975
The U.S. Department of Health, Education and Welfare reports that suicide rates among white females aged 15 through 19 are nearly double those of black female teens, compared with 1970 when the rates were equal.

1985
According to the Centers for Disease Control and Prevention, the suicide rate for 15- to 19-year-olds is 9.9 per 100,000 teens, up from 5.9 per 100,000 teens in 1970.

1990
According to the U.S. Department of Health and Human Services, the suicide rate for teens aged 15 through 19 has nearly doubled since 1970.

1940 **1950** **1975** **1985** **1995**

1942
American psychologist Carl Rogers publishes *Counseling and Psychotherapy*, in which he opines that respect and a nonjudgmental attitude by a psychotherapist is the most effective approach for treatment of mental health problems.

1987
The American Foundation for Suicide Prevention is founded in New York by a group of suicide experts, business and community leaders, and suicide survivors.

1997
The Centers for Disease Control and Prevention reports that the suicide rate for 15- to 19-year-olds is 9.5 per 100,000 teens, which is a 17 percent decrease from 11.1 per 100,000 teens in 1990.

1998
The World Health Organization reports that suicide represents nearly 2 percent of the worldwide burden of disease and is among the top 3 causes of death for people aged 15 to 34.

1999

The U.S. surgeon general releases *A Call to Action to Prevent Suicide*, a blueprint for preventing suicide in the United States. The report outlines more than a dozen steps that can be taken to prevent youth and adult suicides.

2010

The National Center for Health Statistics reports that suicide is the third leading cause of death for teenagers in the United States, after accidental injuries and homicide.

2004

The U.S. Food and Drug Administration issues its most serious "black box" warning for all antidepressant drugs due to the potential risk of increased suicidal thoughts and behaviors among children and adolescents.

2007

The Centers for Disease Control and Prevention reports that after a steady decline between 1990 and 2003, the suicide rate for 10- to 24-year-olds increased by 8 percent between 2003 and 2004, the largest single-year rise in 15 years.

2000

2010

2001

The Youth Suicide Prevention Program is founded in Seattle, Washington.

2005

The Substance Abuse and Mental Health Services Administration awards $5.6 million in grants to 14 states to develop youth suicide prevention and early intervention programs and to 20 colleges to enhance behavioral health services.

2006

Missouri teenager Megan Meier commits suicide after being repeatedly bullied on MySpace. Her death sparks a national outcry for better protection for young people and prompts the introduction of state and federal cyberbullying legislation.

2009

U.S. representative Linda Sanchez introduces the Megan Meier Cyberbullying Prevention Act, which would make it a federal crime to harass, intimidate, or cause substantial emotional stress to someone using electronic media.

Related Organizations

American Association of Suicidology

5221 Wisconsin Ave. NW
Washington, DC 20015
phone: (202) 237-2280 • fax: (202) 237-2282
website: www.suicidology.org

The goal of the American Association of Suicidology is to better understand and prevent suicide. Its website offers fact sheets, statistics, a section on warning signs, and special areas for people who have lost someone to suicide or whose loved one has attempted suicide.

American Foundation for Suicide Prevention

120 Wall St., 22nd Floor
New York, NY 10005
phone: (212) 363-3500; toll-free: (888) 333-2377
fax: (212) 363-6237
e-mail: inquiry@afsp.org • website: www.afsp.org

The American Foundation for Suicide Prevention seeks to prevent suicide through research, education, and advocacy. Its website features the *Lifesavers* newsletter and an "About Suicide" section that covers facts and figures, risk factors, warning signs, and frequently asked questions about suicide.

International Association for Suicide Prevention

National Centre for Suicide Research and Prevention
Sognsvannsveien 21, Bygg 12
N-0372 Oslo, Norway
phone: (47) 229 237 15 • fax: (47) 229 239 58
e-mail: office@iasp.info • website: www.iasp.info

The International Association for Suicide Prevention seeks to prevent suicidal behavior and provide a forum for academics, mental health professionals, crisis workers, and suicide survivors. Its website features archived newsletters, a number of suicide papers, a "Groups at Risk" section, and links to resources for teens and young adults.

Jason Foundation

18 Volunteer Dr.
Hendersonville, TN 37075
phone: (615) 264-2323; toll-free: (888) 881-2323
e-mail: contact@jasonfoundation.com
website: www.jasonfoundation.com

Founded in memory of Jason Flatt, who committed suicide at the age of 16, the Jason Foundation seeks to prevent youth suicide through education and awareness programs. Its website offers facts and figures, risk factors, warning signs, and links to other resources.

Mental Health America

2000 N. Beauregard St., 6th Floor
Alexandria, VA 22311
phone: (703) 684-7722; toll-free: (800) 969-6642
fax: (703) 684-5968
website: www.nmha.org

Mental Health America is dedicated to helping people live mentally healthier lives and to educating the public about mental health and mental illness. Its website features fact sheets and a search engine that produces numerous articles about depression and suicide.

Minding Your Mind Foundation

42 W. Lancaster Ave., 2nd Floor
Ardmore, PA 19003
phone: (610) 642-3879 • fax: (610) 896-5704
website: www.mindingyourmind.org

The Minding Your Mind Foundation provides mental health education to adolescents and seeks to decrease the stigma attached to mental illness. Its website features a "Mental Health Basics" section, statistics, videos, and personal stories of young people who have struggled with mental illness.

National Alliance on Mental Illness (NAMI)

3803 N. Fairfax Dr., Suite 100
Arlington, VA 22203
phone: (703) 524-7600; toll-free: (800) 950-6264
fax: (703) 524-9094
website: www.nami.org

NAMI is dedicated to improving the lives of people who suffer from mental illness, as well as the lives of their families. Its website features fact sheets, videos, online discussion groups, an extensive Mental Illness section that covers teen suicide, the *Advocate* online magazine, and a link to the NAMI blog.

National Institute of Mental Health (NIMH)

Science Writing, Press, and Dissemination Branch
6001 Executive Blvd., Room 8184, MSC 9663
Bethesda, MD 20892-9663
phone: (301) 443-4513; toll-free: (866) 615-6464
fax: (301) 443-4279
e-mail: nimhinfo@nih.gov • website: www.nimh.nih.gov

An agency of the U.S. government, the NIMH is the largest scientific organization in the world specializing in mental illness research and the promotion of mental health. Its website features statistics, archived *Science News* articles, and numerous publications related to suicide.

Society for the Prevention of Teen Suicide

PO Box 6835
Freehold, NJ 07728
phone: (973) 292-0602, ext. 3
e-mail: info@sptsnj.org • website: www.sptsnj.org

Founded by two fathers who lost teens to suicide, the Society for the Prevention of Teen Suicide develops and implements youth suicide prevention programs at both the state and national level. Its website offers a section containing frequently asked questions, separate sections designed for teens, parents, and educators, and links to other resources.

Substance Abuse and Mental Health Services Administration (SAMHSA)

1 Choke Cherry Rd.
Rockville, MD 20857
phone: (877) 726-4727 • fax: (240) 221-4292
e-mail: samhsainfo@samhsa.hhs.gov • website: www.samhsa.gov

The mission of SAMHSA is to reduce the impact of substance abuse and mental illness on America's communities. Its website features a wealth of information about mental health issues and suicide accessible through alphabetized databases or the site's search engine.

Suicide Prevention Action Network

1010 Vermont Ave. NW, Suite 408
Washington, DC 20005
phone: (202) 449-3600 • fax: (202) 449-3601
e-mail: jmadigan@afsp.org • website: www.spanusa.org

The Suicide Prevention Action Network seeks to reduce loss of life from suicide by supporting research, educational campaigns, and policy initiatives. Its website features suicide facts, survivor stories, archived news articles, and legislative updates.

Suicide Prevention Resource Center

Education Development Center, Inc.
55 Chapel St.
Newton, MA 02458-1060
phone: (877) 438-7772 • fax: (617) 969-9186
e-mail: info@sprc.org • website: www.sprc.org

The Suicide Prevention Resource Center supports organizations and individuals in the development of suicide prevention programs, interventions, and policies. Its website offers a glossary of mental health/suicide prevention terms; various publications, including an online newsletter; and news article highlights.

To Write Love on Her Arms

PO Box 206
Cocoa, FL 32923
phone: (321) 735-0228 • fax: (321) 433-3185
e-mail: info@twloha.com • website: www.twloha.com

To Write Love on Her Arms is a nonprofit movement that is dedicated to helping those struggling with depression, addiction, self-injury, and suicide. Its website offers facts, news articles, inspirational messages, a "Find Help" section, a list of recommended books, and a link to a blog.

Trevor Project

Administrative Offices
9056 Santa Monica Blvd., Suite 208
West Hollywood, CA 90069
phone: (310) 271-8845 • fax: (310) 271-8846
e-mail: info@thetrevorproject.org • website: www.thetrevorproject.org

The Trevor Project seeks to promote acceptance of lesbian, gay, bisexual, and transgender youth and to aid in suicide prevention among that group. Its website offers news articles, interactive features, a "Dear Trevor" question and answer resource, a quarterly online newsletter, and a link to the video presentation *It Gets Better*.

Youth Suicide Prevention Program

444 NE Ravenna Blvd., Suite 401
Seattle, WA 98115
phone: (206) 297-5922 • fax: (206) 297-0818
e-mail: info@yspp.org • website: www.yspp.org

The Youth Suicide Prevention Program seeks to end teen suicide by increasing the public's awareness of the problem, as well as educating families about risk factors and effective prevention measures. The website offers publications related to teen suicide, news releases, statistics, frequently asked questions, and links to additional resources.

For Further Research

Books

Donna Holland Barnes, *The Truth About Suicide*. New York: Facts On File, 2010.

Bev Cobain, *When Nothing Matters Anymore*. Minneapolis: Free Spirit, 2007.

Sandra Giddens, *Frequently Asked Questions About Suicide*. New York: Rosen, 2009.

Stephen Hinshaw and Rachel Kranz, *The Triple Bind: Saving Our Teenage Girls from Today's Pressures*. New York: Ballantine, 2009.

Mike Linderman, *The Teen Whisperer: How to Break Through the Silence and Secrecy of Teenage Life*. New York: HarperCollins, 2008.

Gary E. Nelson, *A Relentless Hope: Surviving the Storm of Teen Depression*. Eugene, OR: Cascade, 2007.

Richard E. Nelson and Judith C. Galas, *The Power to Prevent Suicide: A Guide for Teens Helping Teens*. Strawberry Hills, New South Wales, Australia: ReadHowYouWant, 2009.

Lisa M. Schab, *Beyond the Blues: A Workbook to Help Teens Overcome Depression*. Oakland, CA: Instant Help, 2008.

Heidi Williams, ed., *Teen Suicide*. Farmington Hills, MI: Greenhaven, 2009.

Kim Wohlenhaus, *Suicide Information for Teens: Health Tips About Suicide Causes and Prevention*. Detroit: Omnigraphics, 2010.

Carolyn Zahnow, *Save the Teens: Preventing Suicide, Depression, and Addiction*. Snow Camp, NC: Brand New Day, 2010.

Periodicals

Kevin Cullen, "The Untouchable Mean Girls," *Boston Globe*, January 24, 2010.

Tony Dokoupil, "Trouble in a 'Black Box': Did an Effort to Reduce Teen Suicides Backfire?" *Newsweek*, July 16, 2007.

Erik Eckholm and Katie Zezima, "6 Teenagers Are Charged After Classmate's Suicide," *New York Times*, March 29, 2010.

Sarah Wassner Flynn, "Coming Out of the Darkness," *Girls' Life*, December/January 2009.

Gayle Forman, "The Tragic Mystery of Suicide," *Cosmopolitan*, May 2008.

John Keilman, "Fragile Teen Is Saved by Caring and Luck," *Chicago Tribune*, September 20, 2010.

Stacy Teicher Khadaroo, "Suicide Prevention Program Focuses on Teens," *Christian Science Monitor*, January 3, 2008.

Kathy Matheson, "Rare Teen Suicide Pact Leaves Lots of Questions in Interboro Towns," *Delaware County (PA) Daily Times*, March 5, 2010.

Mary Knox Merrill, "Bullying and Teen Suicide: How Do We Adjust School Climate?" *Christian Science Monitor*, April 28, 2010.

Steve Mills and Louise Kiernan, "Suicides Expose Safety Breakdowns, *Chicago Tribune*, May 25, 2010.

Rod Nordland, "A Welsh Teen Suicide Epidemic," *Newsweek*, February 29, 2008.

Mike Stobbe, "Surprising Fact: Half of Gun Deaths Are Suicides," *New York Sun*, July 1, 2008.

Michael Vitez, "After Leap Breaks Body, a Miracle Renews Spirit," *Philadelphia Inquirer*, January 20, 2008.

Eilene Zimmerman, "Teen Angst Turns Deadly: Why Girls Are Killing Themselves," *Psychology Today*, January 2009.

Internet Sources

American Academy of Child & Adolescent Psychiatry, "Teen Suicide," *Facts for Families*, May 2008. http://aacap.org/page.ww?name=Teen +Suicide&section=Facts+for+Families.

Madelyn S. Gould, "Growing Pains: Adolescent Suicide Rates Raise Concerns," interviewed by HealthyPlace, March 17, 2010. www. healthyplace.com/depression/nimh/preventing-suicide-individual-acts-create-a-public-health-crisis/menu-id-1419.

Cristian Salazar, "Alexis Pilkington Facebook Horror: Cyberbullies Harass Teen Even After Suicide," *Huffington Post*, March 24, 2010. www.huffingtonpost.com/2010/03/24/alexis-pilkington-faceboo_n_512482.html.

Brian Slodysko, "Covering Teen Suicide," Dart Center for Journalism and Trauma, April 6, 2009. http://dartcenter.org/content/covering-teen-suicide.

Substance Abuse and Mental Health Services Administration, "Suicide Prevention," *SAMHSA News*, January–February 2009. www.samhsa.gov/samhsaNewsletter/Volume_17_Number_1/JanuaryFebruary2009.pdf.

U.S. Department of Health and Human Services, "Stop Bullying Now!" www.stopbullyingnow.hrsa.gov.

Source Notes

Overview

1. Quoted in Suzie Schottelkotte, "Detectives Rule Fatal Haven Crash a Suicide," *Lakeland (FL) Ledger*, July 28, 2009. www.theledger.com.
2. Quoted in Schottelkotte, "Detectives Rule Fatal Haven Crash a Suicide."
3. Parliamentary Assembly of the Council of Europe, *Child and Teenage Suicide in Europe: A Serious Public-Health Issue*, March 27, 2008. http://assembly.coe.int.
4. Substance Abuse and Mental Health Services Administration, "Know the Warning Signs—Prevent Suicide in Young People," August 28, 2007. http://family.samhsa.gov.
5. Centers for Disease Control and Prevention, "Risk Factors for Suicide," *Suicide: Risk and Protective Factors*, August 31, 2010. www.cdc.gov.
6. Madelyn S. Gould, "Growing Pains: Adolescent Suicide Rates Raise Concerns," interviewed by HealthyPlace, March 17, 2010. www.healthyplace.com.
7. American Academy of Child & Adolescent Psychiatry, "Teen Suicide," *Facts for Families*, May 2008. www.aacap.org.
8. Quoted in John Keilman, "Fragile Teen Is Saved by Caring and Luck," *Chicago Tribune*, September 10, 2010. http://articles.chicagotribune.com.
9. Jim Wellborn, "There's a Stranger in My House," *Brentwood Home Page*, October 4, 2010. http://brentwoodhomepage.com.
10. Wellborn, "There's a Stranger in My House."
11. Harold Koplewicz, "Suicide and the Antidepressant Question," *Huffington Post*, March 9, 2010. www.huffingtonpost.com.
12. Quoted in *Huffington Post*, "Michael Blosil, Osmond Son: Friends Share Memories, Talk Night of Suicide," March 1, 2010. www.huffingtonpost.com.
13. Stan Kid, e-mail interview with author, October 11, 2010.
14. Yilmaz Yildirim, Ummuhan Yesil-Dagli, and Richard Bloch, "Prevalence of Mental Illness and Substance Abuse Among Child and Adolescent Suicide Victims," *New Research Abstracts to the 2010 Annual Meeting*, American Psychiatric Association, May 2010. www.psych.org.
15. Steve Gerali, interviewed by R.J. Carter, "Interview: Dr. Steve Gerali: To Save a Life," Trades, September 10, 2010. www.the-trades.com.
16. Phil McGraw, "Bullied to Death," *Turning Point: Home of Dr. Phil's Official Blog*, October 5, 2010. http://blog.drphil.com.
17. Paul Butler, "Not Every Tragedy Should Lead to Prison," Room for Debate, *New York Times*, September 30, 2010. www.nytimes.com.
18. National Alliance on Mental Illness, "Teenage Suicide." www.nami.org.
19. National Alliance on Mental Illness, "Teenage Suicide."

How Serious a Problem Is Teenage Suicide?

20. American Academy of Child & Adolescent Psychiatry, "Your Adolescent—Depressive Disorders," 2009. www.aacap.org.
21. Quoted in Salynn Boyles, "Teens, Parents Underestimate Suicide Risk,"

MedicineNet, January 11, 2010. www.medicinenet.com.

22. Centers for Disease Control and Prevention, "Suicide Prevention: Youth Suicide," October 15, 2009. www.cdc.gov.

23. Quoted in Selena Roberts, "A Young Man's Fall to Grace," *Sports Illustrated*, May 17, 2010. http://sportsillustrated.cnn.com.

24. Quoted in Roberts, "A Young Man's Fall to Grace."

25. Jordan Burnham, *Life After the Fall*, blog, Minding Your Mind Foundation, December 30, 2008. http://blogs.mindingyourmind.org.

26. Gould, "Growing Pains."

27. Alex Shoumatoff, "The Mystery Suicides of Bridgend County," *Vanity Fair*, February 27, 2009. www.vanityfair.com.

28. Quoted in Carole Cadwalladr, "How Bridgend Was Damned by Distortion," *Observer*, March 1, 2009. www.guardian.co.uk.

29. Quoted in Christine Kim, "State Leaders Discuss the Problem of Teen Suicide," KTUU-TV, October 5, 2010. www.ktuu.com.

Why Do Teenagers Take Their Own Lives?

30. Quoted in Joseph Rizza, "Turning Tragedy into Triumph: Paula Pilkington Speaks About Daughter, Depression," *West Islip (NY) Patch*, July 19, 2010. http://westislip.patch.com.

31. American Academy of Pediatrics, "Parenting Corner Q&A: What Are the Warning Signs of Suicide?" February 2007. www.aap.org.

32. National Institute of Mental Health, *Bipolar Disorder in Children and Teens: A Parent's Guide*, August 31, 2010. www.nimh.nih.gov.

33. Quoted in Rasha Madkour, "Report:

Teen Commits Suicide Online," MSNBC, November 21, 2008. www.msnbc.msn.com.

34. Deb Martinson, "Self-Injury: Fact Sheet (Beyond the Myths)," eNotAlone, 2009. www.enotalone.com.

35. Sylvermoon, "I Can't Fight the Urge," *Self-Injury Support Group*, discussion group, DailyStrength, October 3, 2009. www.dailystrength.org.

36. Quoted in Kim Marquis, "The Quiet Tragedy: Teen Suicide in Juneau," *Juneau (AK) Empire*, March 30, 2008. www.juneauempire.com.

37. University of Denver Graduate School of Social Work, "Stacey Freedenthal," September 2007. www.du.edu.

38. Stacey Freedenthal, Michael G. Vaughn, Jeffrey M. Jenson, and Matthew O. Howard, *Inhalant Use and Suicidality Among Incarcerated Youth*, National Institutes of Health, September 6, 2007. www.ncbi.nlm.nih.gov.

39. Youth Suicide Prevention Program, "Youth Suicide Frequently Asked Questions (FAQ)." www.yspp.org.

Does Bullying Drive Teenagers to Suicide?

40. Kid, interview.

41. Tom Harrison, telephone interview with author, October 27, 2010.

42. Harrison, interview.

43. Quoted in KLAS-TV 8 News NOW, "Anti-Bullying Rally Held for Students," October 5, 2010. www.8newsnow.com.

44. Quoted in Patricia Reaney, "Cyberbullying, More than Just 'Messing Around,'" *Vancouver Sun*, May 12, 2009. www.vancouversun.com.

45. Gerali, "Interview."

46. Quoted in Cindy Kranz, "Nude Photo Led to Suicide," Cincinnati.com, March 22, 2009. http://news.cincinnati.com.

47. Cynthia Logan, MSNBC *Today* appearance, March 6, 2009. http://today.msnbc.msn.com.

48. Ken Trump, "Bullycide: Death by Bullying or Deeper Mental Health Issues?," School Security Blog, September 2010. www.schoolsecurityblog.com.

49. Harrison, interview.

50. Harold Koplewicz, "Combating Gay Teen Suicide: What Parents Can Do," *Huffington Post*, October 14, 2010. www.huffingtonpost.com.

51. Quoted in Alison Gendar, Edgar Sandoval, and Larry McShane, "Rutgers Freshman Kills Self After Classmates Use Hidden Camera to Watch His Sexual Activity: Sources," *New York Daily News*, September 30, 2010. www.nydailynews.com.

52. Quoted in Gendar et al., "Rutgers Freshman Kills Self After Classmates Use Hidden Camera to Watch His Sexual Activity."

53. Pk Harrison, posted on the Facebook page "In Loving Memory of Alex Harrison," June 21, 2010. www.facebook.com.

Can Teenage Suicide Be Stopped?

54. Quoted in Keilman, "Fragile Teen Is Saved by Caring and Luck."

55. Quoted in Keilman, "Fragile Teen Is Saved by Caring and Luck."

56. Quoted in Keilman, "Fragile Teen Is Saved by Caring and Luck."

57. Quoted in Keilman, "Fragile Teen Is Saved by Caring and Luck."

58. HealthyPlace staff, "How to Handle a Suicide Threat—for Teens," reviewed by psychiatrist Harry Croft, Healthy Place, December 22, 2008. www.healthyplace.com.

59. Mary, e-mail interview with author, October 26, 2010.

60. Quoted in Julie Williams, "Responding to Teen Suicide: What You Need to Know," Education.com, February 16, 2010. www.education.com.

61. HealthyPlace staff, "Emerging Teen-Depression Treatment Teaches Kids How to Handle Anxiety," reviewed by psychiatrist Harry Croft, HealthyPlace, December 9, 2008. www.healthyplace.com.

62. Quoted in HealthyPlace staff, "Emerging Teen-Depression Treatment Teaches Kids How to Handle Anxiety."

63. Quoted in Rick Nauert, "Family Therapy Helps Suicidal Teens," Psych Central, February 8, 2010. http://psychcentral.com.

64. Substance Abuse and Mental Health Services Administration, *Substance Abuse and Suicide Prevention: Evidence & Implications*, 2008. http://store.samhsa.gov.

65. Laurie L. Levenson, "What Isn't Known About Suicides," Room for Debate, *New York Times*, September 30, 2010. www.nytimes.com.

66. Levenson, "What Isn't Known About Suicides."

67. Quoted in Rizza, "Turning Tragedy into Triumph."

List of Illustrations

Index

Note: Page numbers in boldface
indicate illustrations.

Index

About the Author

Peggy J. Parks holds a bachelor of science degree from Aquinas College in Grand Rapids, Michigan, where she graduated magna cum laude. An author who has written more than 100 educational books for children and young adults, Parks lives in Muskegon, Michigan, a town that she says inspires her writing because of its location on the shores of Lake Michigan.

Date Due
